Art Editor Toni Rann
Senior Editor Jane Yorke
Photography Stephen Oliver
Series Consultant Neil Morris
Editorial Director Sue Unstead
Art Director Anne-Marie Bulat

This is a Dorling Kindersley Book
published by Random House, Inc.

First American edition, 1990
10th printing

Library of Congress Cataloging-in-Publication Data
My first look at colors.
    p.   cm.
    Published also under title: Colours
    Summary: Photographs explore the concept of color,
from red cherries and yellow duck to blue marbles
and other colorful objects.
    ISBN 0-679-80535-4
    1. Colors - Juvenile literature. 2. Color - Juvenile literature.
[1. Color.] I. Random House (Firm)
QC495.M95 1990
535.6 - dc20 89-63091 CIP AC

Manufactured in Italy   10

Phototypeset by Windsorgraphics, Ringwood, Hampshire
Reproduced in Hong Kong by Bright Arts
Printed in Italy by L.E.G.O.

· MY · FIRST · LOOK · AT ·
Colors

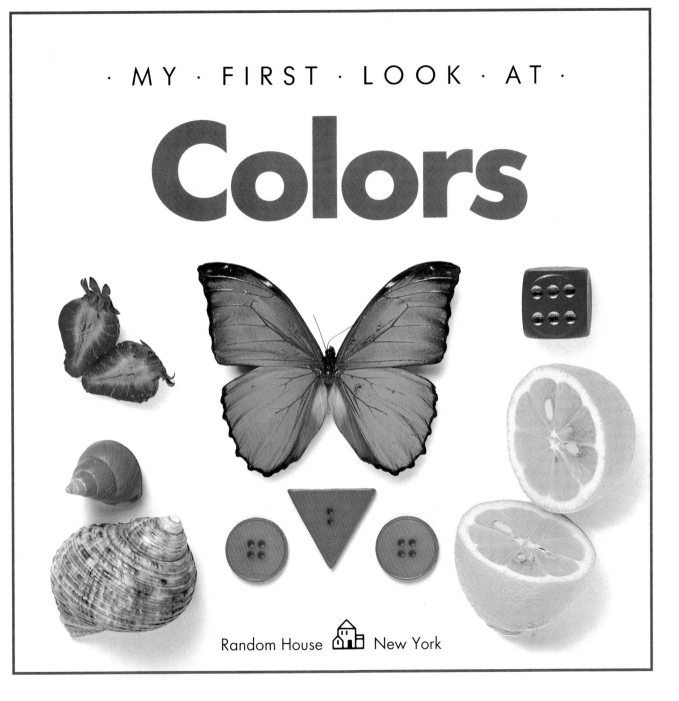

Random House 🏠 New York

Red

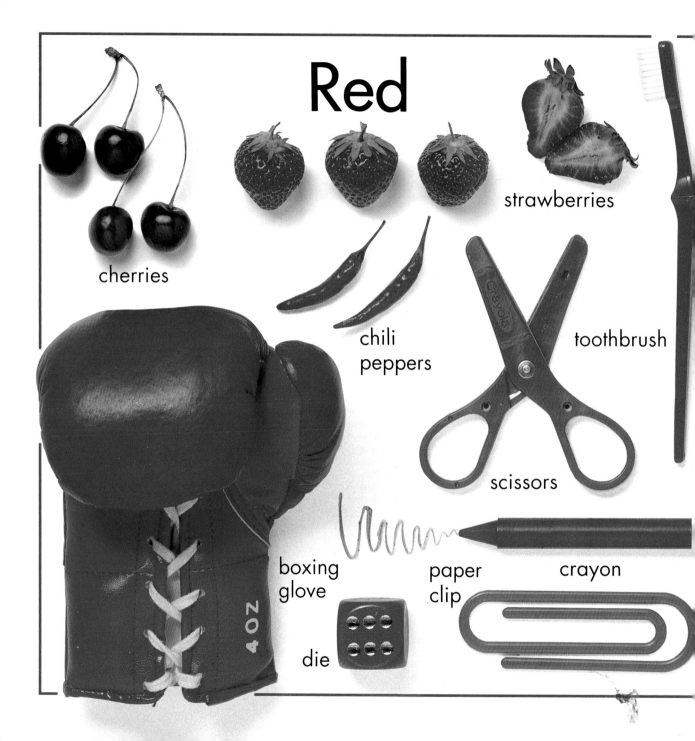

cherries

strawberries

chili
peppers

toothbrush

scissors

boxing
glove

paper
clip

crayon

die

baby cup

fork
and
knife

lipstick

sock

apple

rose

boot

car

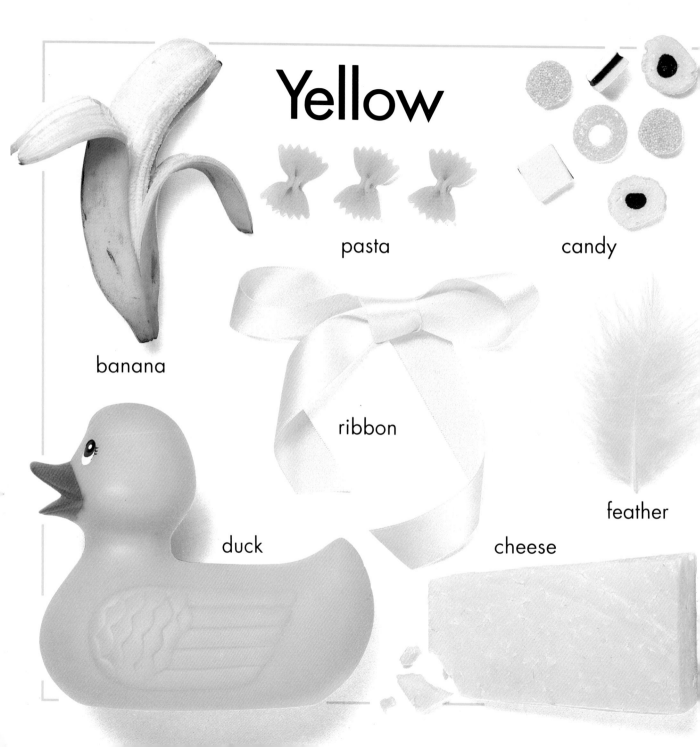

Yellow

pasta

candy

banana

ribbon

feather

duck

cheese

brush

comb

sponge

lemon

balloon

daffodil

teddy
bear

blocks

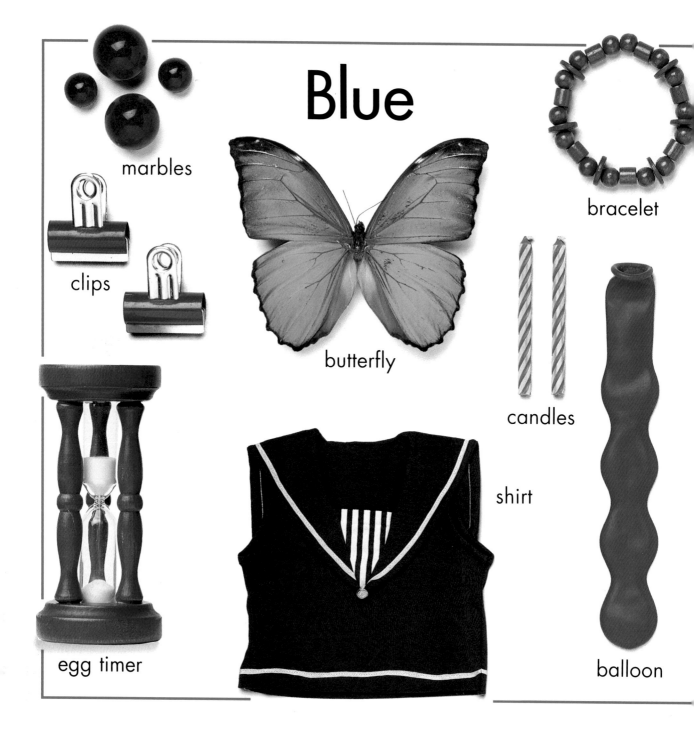

Blue

marbles

bracelet

clips

butterfly

candles

egg timer

shirt

balloon

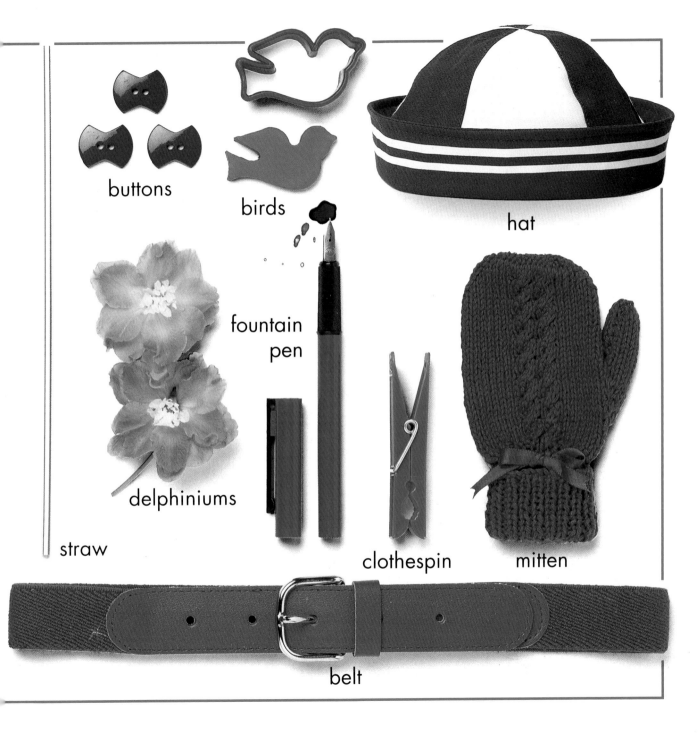

buttons

birds

hat

fountain
pen

delphiniums

straw

clothespin

mitten

belt

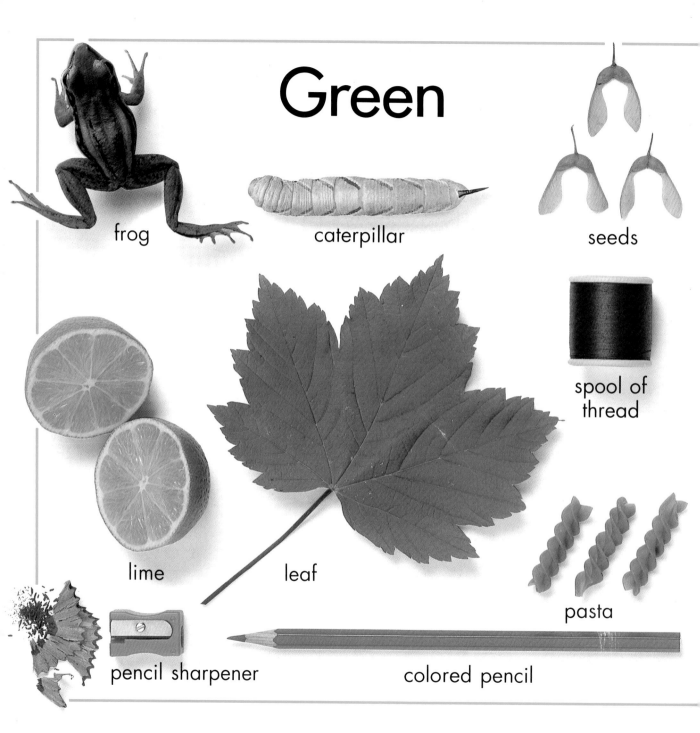

Green

frog

caterpillar

seeds

lime

leaf

spool of thread

pasta

pencil sharpener

colored pencil

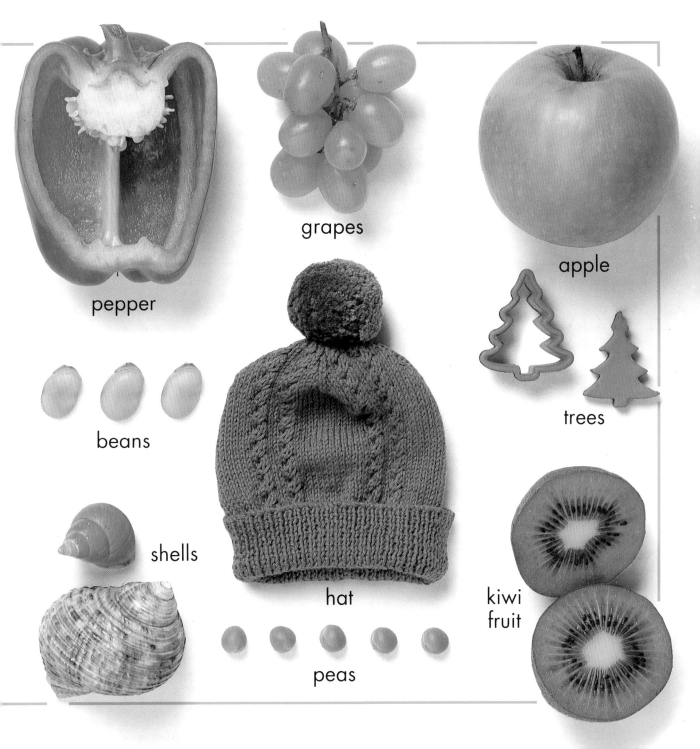

pepper

grapes

apple

beans

trees

shells

hat

kiwi
fruit

peas

Orange

shell

starfish

carrots

apricot jam

crab

ball

buttons

ice pop

candy
cane

soaps

orange

paint

goldfish

shovel

lily

pail

Pink

shrimp

beads

coral

safety pins

cake

cotton balls

ballet slippers

soaps

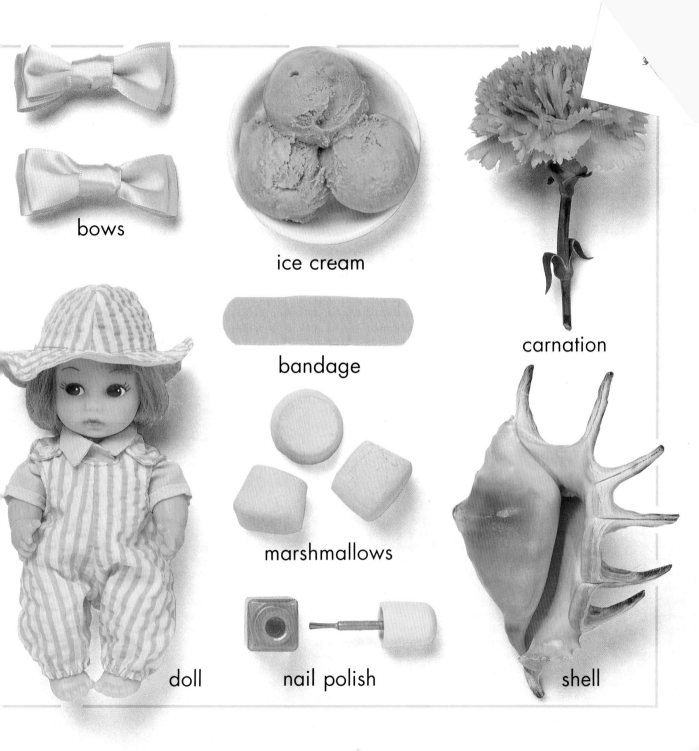

bows

ice cream

carnation

bandage

doll

marshmallows

nail polish

shell

Brown

onions

bird's eggs

leaf

colored pencils

pine cones

feather

caramels

gingerbread man

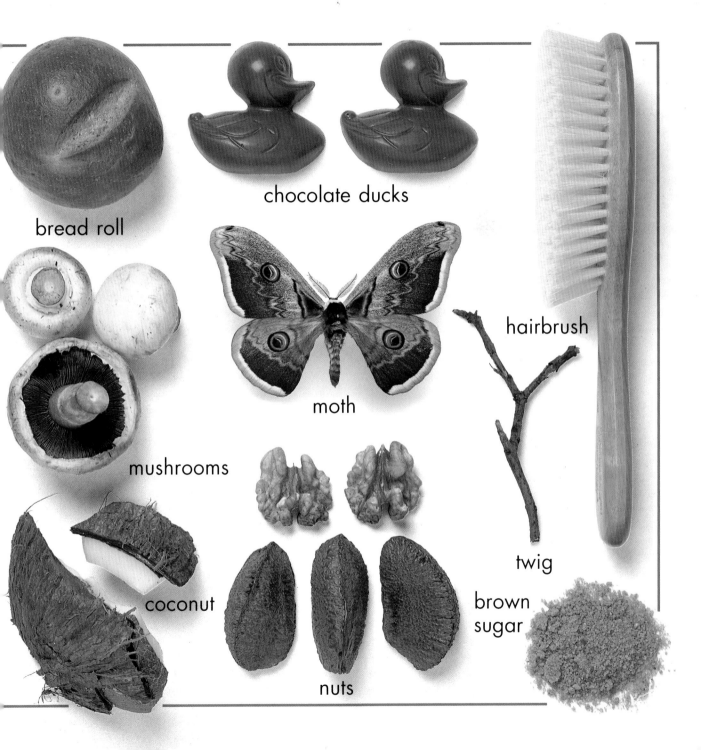

bread roll

chocolate ducks

hairbrush

moth

mushrooms

twig

coconut

nuts

brown
sugar

Black and white

licorice

coal

olives

beetle

bracelet

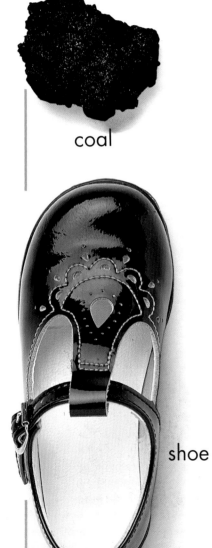

shoe

bow tie

purse

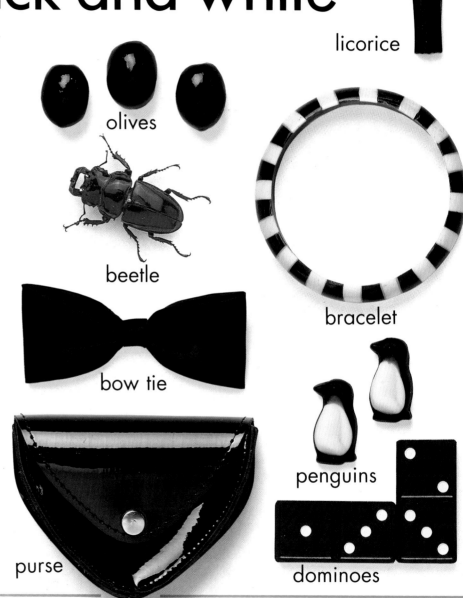

penguins

dominoes

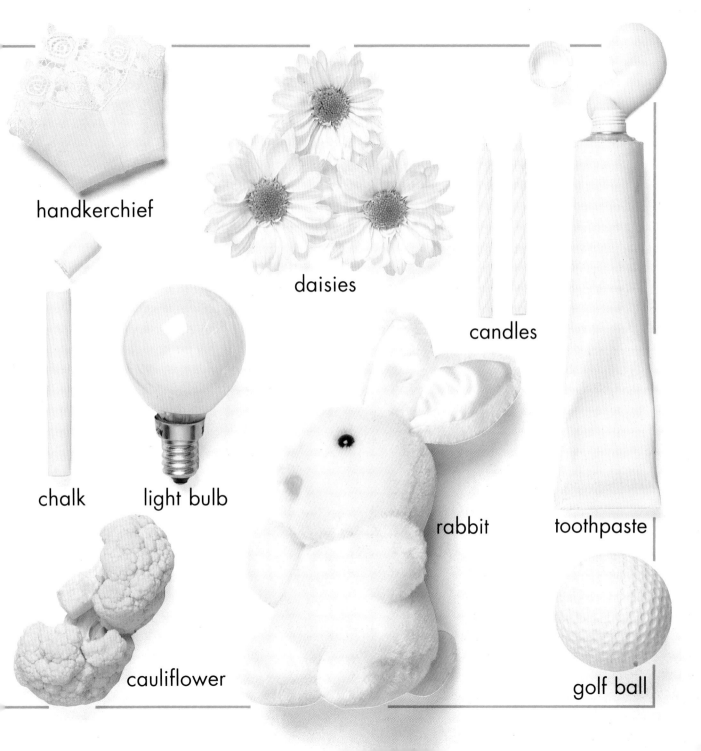

handkerchief

daisies

candles

chalk   light bulb

rabbit

toothpaste

cauliflower

golf ball